THEY LED THE WAY

14 American Women
(Original title: Women Themselves)

by Johanna Johnston

Inside illustrations
by Deanne Hollinger

SCHOLASTIC INC.
New York Toronto London Auckland Sydney

ISBN 0-590-44431-X

Text copyright © 1973 by Johanna Johnston. Illustrations copyright © 1973 by Deanne Hollinger. All rights reserved. This edition published by Scholastic Inc., 730 Broadway, New York, NY 10003, by arrangement with Dodd, Mead & Co., Inc.

24 23 22 21 20 19 18 17 16 15 14 13   6 7/9

Printed in the U.S.A.   40

For all the countless women,
unmentioned in this book,
each of whom in her own way
dared to be herself.

Contents

Women in Their Place

Of course women were there.
As soon as the men of Europe
began settling in the New World,
women were with them,
doing what women were supposed to do.

While the men were out clearing land,
hunting, or exploring,
trading, or fighting with Indians,
the women were cooking, washing,
planting gardens,
and taking care of children.

While the men were laying out towns,
building houses,
making laws, and deciding how people
who broke the laws should be punished,

the women were preserving food for winter,
cleaning house,
and making soap and candles.

The men preached sermons and told
people how God wished them to behave,
and the women listened—
and cooked and washed and sewed
and took care of children.

As far as men were concerned
that was all women were meant to do.
Their place was in the home
and they were not supposed to have
anything to say about important matters,
like the making of laws,
the need for fighting or making peace,
or what ways of behaving *they* thought
might be most pleasing to God.

But from the beginning

there were many women of intelligence
among the settlers of America.
There were women
who thought for themselves,
and women
who had talents they wanted to use.

The women who wanted to speak out
about what they thought,
the women who wanted to use their talents
for something more than cooking and cleaning,
needed a very special determination.

The wonder is how many there were
who were not content to stay in their places,
but insisted on being all that they could be.

This book tells about just a few
of those women.

Anne Hutchinson *(1591-1643)*

On Trial for Thinking for Herself

A woman—*preaching*? The men in the little town of Boston looked at each other in horror as the news went from one to another. Was it possible?

"It could be," said one man. "My wife goes one afternoon each week to the home of Mistress Anne Hutchinson, and she comes back very thoughtful."

Another man said, "My wife does the same."

Still another said, "Half the women in Boston go to Mistress Hutchinson's one afternoon each week. It is true, they take their sewing and quilting. But I do hear

that Mistress Hutchinson talks about the Sunday sermons."

Another said, "She does more than that. My wife let it fall that Mistress Hutchinson says we Puritans are too hard on people of other faiths. She says also that we should not use Indians as slaves."

Some of the others cried out, "*What?*"

The man went on. "Yes, yes, and I think she has other dangerous views, but when my wife saw my face she would say no more."

"This must be stopped!" said one of the men. "How dares a woman put forth such ideas?" Soon they decided that one of Boston's most important preachers, the Reverend John Cotton, should speak to Anne Hutchinson.

"Is it true?" the Reverend Cotton asked Anne Hutchinson. "Are you preaching to the women at these afternoon meetings?"

Anne Hutchinson shook her head. She was a small, lively person who admired the Reverend Cotton very much. In fact, she and her husband had left England and brought their family to America to settle in Boston just because the Reverend Cotton had done so.

"Oh no, sir," she said, "you could *never* call it preaching. I talk — we all talk — about the Sunday sermons. We study the Bible. And sometimes I try to explain some of its words when it seems that God has given me a sign."

The Reverend Cotton looked shocked. "You think that God gives *you* signs?" Anne Hutchinson nodded. The Reverend Cotton said, "But this is terrible. Only ministers can receive signs from

God. Certainly no woman can. Say you are mistaken. Otherwise you must be tried by the court. You may be sent away from Boston. Say you were mistaken."

But this was something Anne Hutchinson could not do. She had always been a person who thought for herself, even when she was a small girl in England. She could not help thinking for herself now and speaking about what she thought.

And so Anne Hutchinson was brought to trial before a group of ministers. She stood before them bravely and tried to prove, with words from the Bible, that women, as well as men, might receive signs from God, and that women, as well as men, had the right to speak their thoughts. But the more she said the more the ministers turned against her. At the end of her trial, they sentenced her to be banished from the Massachusetts colony.

Anne Hutchinson and her family did not have an easy time after that. They stayed for a while in the Rhode Island colony. Then they traveled into the New York colony and settled there. And there, the cruelest thing of all happened. Anne Hutchinson had always been friendly with Indians. But one day, some hot-tempered braves, who did not know Anne Hutchinson, killed her and all her children but one.

Still, her courage to say what she thought had not been in vain. Many people in Boston who had heard her talk remembered what she had said. Gradually, they began to think she had been right about many things—and they made some changes in Puritan ways.

Some history books do mention her

name. It is remembered in other places too. A river in New York, near which she lived, is called the Hutchinson River, after her. The highway that runs along it is called the Hutchinson River Parkway —after Anne Hutchinson, a woman who did what she wasn't supposed to.

Anne Bradstreet *(1612-1672)*

First Poet in Colonial America

She woke in the night to hear someone crying, "Fire! Fire!" In a second, Anne Bradstreet was out of bed. Now she could smell smoke and hear the crackling of wood. She reached into the cradle beside her bed and lifted out the baby. She ran into the next room, calling the names of her older children. "Get up! Get up quickly!" she cried.

Soon Anne Bradstreet was pushing her

children out through the door into the warm, windy night. The flames of their burning house made the sky red. Some neighbors ran to them to make sure they were all right. Others were running from the well to the house with buckets of water. But it was too late to put out this fire. As they watched the roof fell in, and the house became a heap of burning rubble.

It was a hard blow to Anne Bradstreet. She thought of how long it had taken to build this house. She thought of how her husband would feel when he came home to Andover from his trip to Boston. Then she looked at her children and smiled. Nothing that really mattered was lost. She began to think what she must do next.

There was much to be done. It was

some time before Anne Bradstreet began to write a poem. A poem? Yes.

Anne Bradstreet could no more help writing poems than a bird can help singing. She had written poems to tell her love for her husband . . .

If ever two were one, then surely we.
If ever man were lov'd by wife, then
    thee . . .

She had written poems about her children too, and the happy life of her family. Now she wrote about the fire.

In silent night when rest I took,
For sorrow near I did not look. . . .

Then she went on to tell about the frightening happenings of the night.

Anne Bradstreet was fortunate. Nobody said, "You are not supposed to write poems. You are a woman, a wife, a mother. Leave poetry for men to write."

Anne Bradstreet's husband, Simon, was a generous, intelligent man. He thought his wife's poems were beautiful.

And so it happened that when Simon's brother had to make a trip to England, he took along a number of Anne's poems. He found that the people in England admired them also. Someone said they should be put into a book. Soon that was done. The little book of Anne Bradstreet's poems became very popular. Hers were the first poems from America that the people of England had ever seen.

Years later, people would discover that the Indians, the very first Americans, had composed many poems. But after their songs, Anne Bradstreet's poems come next in almost every collection of American poetry.

Lady Deborah Moody *(1600-1660)*

Mayor of Her Own Town

"A town of my own," said Lady Deborah Moody, smiling in a sort of wonder. The Dutch Governor of New Amsterdam, William Kieft, looked at the eager woman.

"Mmmmpf," he said. "You have the land now, yes. Building a town on it may not be easy. And remember, I have warned you about the Indians."

Lady Deborah kept smiling. "I am sure I can come to good terms with the Indians," she said. "And I can get the town

built. I will!" She said again in wonder, "A town of my own."

She had never dreamed of such a thing when she set sail from England with her young son, Harry. All she had hoped for then was to find a happy new home for them in America. Her husband had died a few years earlier and left her a wealthy woman with a large manor house and many acres.

But it was lonely at the manor with her husband gone. Lady Deborah liked traveling. She liked people. She also thought of herself as a Puritan. Suddenly she was remembering that hundreds, even thousands, of English Puritans were moving to America. She decided that she and Harry should do so too. She sold her house and lands. She sewed the gold she received into her clothes and

Harry's, and they boarded a ship.

They landed at Boston and it looked like a pleasant town. The people welcomed her and her son. So Lady Deborah bought a house and was ready to be happy.

But soon she learned that her ideas of being a good Puritan were quite different from the ideas of the Boston ministers. She had not had young Harry baptized because she thought the ceremony should wait until children were old enough to understand it.

The ministers were horrified by this and argued with her day after day. Lady Deborah was horrified herself by the harsh way the Puritans treated people of other faiths. She was not happy either about the way they treated Indians or about the laws they had passed to regulate almost every minute of life.

She decided to move to some other town. She had made some friends in Boston who felt as she did and they decided to move with her. The first town they tried was Salem, up the river from Boston. But they had not stayed there long before they found that Salem's Puritans were just as harsh as those of Boston.

Lady Deborah and her friends moved on again. This time they took a small ship and sailed along the New England coast until they came to a settlement on an island at the mouth of the Hudson River. This was New Amsterdam, a town that had been started by the Dutch. By now, some English people lived there also and people from other countries. It was not a Puritan town.

An Englishman showed Lady Deborah

around. They stopped on the riverbank and the Englishman pointed across the river. "Long Island," he said. "The part you see is called Brooklyn by the Dutch. It is rich, unsettled land. I am sure you could buy some if you wished."

Suddenly, Lady Deborah had a wonderful idea. Instead of going from town to town and being disappointed, why not start a town herself and make it what she thought a town should be?

It was a daring idea — but not impossible. She still had some of the gold she had brought from England and from the sale of her Boston house. A few days later, the Dutch Governor, William Kieft, was handing her the deed to a large tract of land on the southwest tip of Long Island, along with permission to start a town there.

She was the first woman in America to

be granted such a permission. But she had no time to wonder about that. She was busy planning her town, with a green in the center and lots for houses all around, joining on fields. She was granting lots to friends who had come with her from Boston, and arranging for building to start. Most important of all, she was writing the laws for her town. It was to be free in every way. There would be no slavery, and people of every faith would be welcome.

Not everything went smoothly. There were storms that slowed the building. The Long Island Indians did try to drive Lady Deborah and her friends away. But Lady Deborah was so generous and fair with them that before long they decided to be friendly.

And finally, there was the town with houses, stockade, and a meeting-house, where Quakers, Baptists, Jews, people of any faith could worship. Lady Deborah called her town Gravesend, after a town she had known in England.

A new Dutch Governor came to rule New Amsterdam — the hot-tempered, one-legged Peter Stuyvesant. When he visited Gravesend and found a woman in charge, he was horrified. A *woman* — the chief authority?

But soon Lady Deborah had won even Peter Stuyvesant's respect. He called her the "Grande Dame of Gravesend." And that was what she was, through all the rest of her busy, happy life.

Gravesend is still part of Brooklyn in New York City. It is a crowded place that Lady Deborah would not recognize. Coney Island, which was also part of her land, is a world-famous beach, and the crowds there would look strange to her also. But the spirit of freedom which Lady Deborah thought so important is still there, just as America's first lady mayor would have wished.

Phillis Wheatley *(1753-1784)*

Honored by General Washington

"This — is — a — book," said Mary Wheatley slowly. She held up a book for the small, black girl to see.

The little girl looked at the book. She

had never seen anything like it. But she wanted to learn about everything in her new, strange life. "Book," she said carefully. "Book."

Only a few days before, she had been hungry, cold, and frightened. She had been sitting on the Boston wharf along with many other black people who had been kidnapped from their African

homes just as she had been. For weeks they had suffered through a terrible ocean voyage. They could see nothing ahead but more suffering. They were slaves, to be sold and ordered about and treated in any way that their masters chose.

And then, for the little girl, the miracle had happened. John Wheatley, a Boston merchant, saw the child. He took pity on her and bought her from the slave trader.

Soon the little girl was in the Wheatley home. Mrs. Wheatley and the two Wheatley children, Mary and Nathaniel, were as kind as Mr. Wheatley. Soon the child was warm, fed, and clothed, and then asleep in a comfortable bed. She woke up to more loving care.

The Wheatleys named her Phillis, for

they could not understand her name nor anything that she tried to tell them in her African speech. But the little girl did not mind being Phillis. If these kind and loving people could not understand her words, she would learn to understand theirs.

"Book," she repeated after Mary. Then she held the book in her hands, and leafed through the pages, looking at the pictures.

Mary said, "Soon I will start teaching you to read." And indeed, before long, Phillis was learning her A B C's. Soon she was reading words and sentences. Then Mary was helping her to read the Bible.

The days and weeks went by and Phillis was part of the Wheatley family. Along with Mary, she helped Mrs.

Wheatley. She learned to cook and spin and weave and do all the things girls and women had to do in those days. She went to church with the family. And all the while she was racing ahead in her studies. She read the Bible through. Then she was reading the works of English poets. She was learning Latin. The Wheatleys were very proud of her.

One day, Mary ran out to the kitchen. "Mother," she said, "I think Phillis is a genius."

Mrs. Wheatley looked up from the dough she was kneading and smiled. "She is certainly very intelligent," she said, "but genius is a big word, Mary."

"Oh, I know," said Mary. "But look, Mother. Here is a poem Phillis wrote. She just showed it to me."

Mrs. Wheatley said, "A poem?"

"Yes," said Mary, "and it is beautiful. Listen.

*'Twas mercy brought me from my
    Pagan land,
Taught my benighted soul to under-
    stand
That there's a God and there's a
    Saviour too...."*

Mary stopped. "Oh, Mother, she's only thirteen, and she can write a poem like that. She *is* a genius."

Mrs. Wheatley, and then Mr. Wheatley too, had to agree with Mary. They were so proud of Phillis that they had the poem printed and showed it to their friends.

"A *black girl* wrote that?" people said. "An African?" "A slave?" "A *girl*?" they said.

"Yes," said the Wheatleys. "A little black girl. But not a slave." They had given Phillis her freedom months before.

"Well," said everyone, wondering. "Think of that. A black *girl*."

Phillis went on to write more poems and the Wheatleys had them printed too. Phillis Wheatley was becoming famous as the first black poet in America. She was invited to England, and Nathaniel, who had business there, took her across the ocean and was proud to see how she was honored everywhere.

They came back to America just as the first battles of the Revolution were being fought. Phillis wrote a poem to George Washington and sent it to him. He wrote back thanking her and inviting her to visit him.

One day in 1776, Phillis did meet and talk with America's general, George Washington. But after that, life became sadder for Phillis. Mr. and Mrs. Wheatley, who had been like father and mother to her, both died. Phillis married a man, John Peters, who was not a good husband. She had to work very hard as a teacher to support them and their children.

Then Phillis herself became ill and died when still very young. But the fame she had won lived on, and her poems did too.

Abigail Adams *(1744-1818)*

Independence Day for Women Too

"My dearest friend," Abigail called her husband in the letters she wrote to him. And John Adams wrote back, calling her "My best, my dearest, my wisest friend." There was great love and understanding between these two.

John was in Philadelphia, Pennsylvania, where men from all the thirteen American colonies were meeting to decide what to do about the hard laws and taxes that England was imposing on them. He wrote to Abigail about the excitement as some men argued that the colonies should make themselves free of England and become independent. John was for independence himself, and he told Abigail why, and asked if she did not agree.

Abigail was at home in Quincy, Massachusetts, taking care of their four children, and managing the farm also, while John was away. So she gave John news of what was happening there and how the children were growing. Then she wrote that she too thought independence would be a good thing. She knew that winning it might be difficult but surely it would be worth a struggle. Their letters went back and forth in the saddlebags of whatever rider was traveling from Philadelphia to Quincy.

One day, Abigail was teaching her two

oldest children to read, when a letter came from John telling her that it was almost certain that the colonies would declare their independence. When that happened, John said, "America will need all sorts of heroes, statesmen, and philosophers."

Abigail looked at her son and daughter—waiting to hear what their

father had written and also to go on with their lessons. She thought of how most children had their first lessons from their mothers. Later, she wrote to John. "If we mean to have heroes, statesmen, and philosophers, we should have learned women."

But she knew many women who had never learned enough to teach their children as she did hers. This was because many men thought that girls should not be educated. Abigail asked John if he did not think that this was wrong. Should not girls be as well educated as boys?

John agreed. He said that of course it would be good if all women were as well educated as his dear Abigail. But then he forgot the matter. He had more exciting things to report. The men in Philadelphia were voting to declare American independence. A great new day was coming. America was to be a land of free men.

Suddenly Abigail was thinking about American *women*. No women were voting in Philadelphia. There was no talk in Philadelphia about a land where women would be just as free as men were. When a woman married, her husband ruled her in every way. When a husband was kind and generous as John was, the wife did not suffer. But Abigail knew many women who had husbands who were tyrants, just like King George III.

She wrote her thoughts to John. Since the men were now deciding that the colonies should be independent, she wondered why they did not also consider the need for *women* to be independent too.

This time, Abigail received an answer that shocked and hurt her. John was laughing at her. He told her that women already had all the power they needed. He said men mostly did what women wanted. But if women wanted *more* power for petticoats, he hoped that General Washington and all of America's heroes would fight them.

Abigail thought that this was the first time that her "dearest friend" had failed her. She wrote to tell him that he was not very generous, and that she thought that some day women would free themselves, just as American men were freeing themselves from English rule. John did not answer that. He dropped the subject.

Abigail did not let her love for John be hurt by this disagreement. The war between the colonies and England was fought and the United States was born.

John Adams was one of America's leaders. Again he was away so much that he and Abigail wrote many letters. Then he became the first Vice-President of the new nation. He and Abigail and their family could be together.

Later still, he became President, and he and Abigail were the first to live in the new White House in Washington, D.C. History books tell of how the White House was still unfinished and Abigail Adams hung the family wash in the East Room to dry.

But we can remember her as more than just a housewife, busy with the laundry. She was a person in her own right, thinking ahead to the day when America would be a land of free *people* — women, as well as men.

Emma Willard *(1787-1870)*

She Started the
First College for Women

Young Emma Hart's parents were delighted. They thought Emma would be
happy too. A new school was opening
nearby, and *girls* could attend as well as
boys. Mr. and Mrs. Hart wanted both
their daughters to go to the new school.
Nancy, the older one, was excited by the
idea. But Emma, the one they thought
would be happiest, said, "Must I go?"

All day long she argued against going.
At night, when her parents had gone to

bed, she came into their room with her candle, still arguing.

"What does a girl need with schooling?" she said. "It's silly. A girl grows up and gets married, and what does she need with history and arithmetic then?"

Her father sighed. "All right," he said. "You do not want to go to the new school. What do you want?"

Emma said, "Oh, what I really want to do is go and visit brother and his family in Kensington." Her brother, who was much older than she, had children with whom Emma always had a good time.

Her parents looked at each other. Then they said, "All right. If that's what you want to do the most."

So Emma went off to visit her brother and had a lovely time. But when she came back, her sister, Nancy, showed her the books she was reading, and told

her about some of her lessons, and suddenly Emma seemed to wake up. These books and lessons were *interesting*. She wanted to know more about them. She ran to her mother.

"Mother," she said, "I am going to school tomorrow."

Mrs. Hart looked at Emma with surprise. "But you think education is silly for girls."

Emma said, "I've changed my mind." And so, the very next day, Emma went off to the new school.

It was just the beginning of Emma's

education. She learned all the arithmetic that the teacher in the school could teach her. But numbers were so interesting to her now that she wanted to learn geometry. She got a book on the subject and learned it by herself. She studied other subjects by herself, or with her father, or with anyone who could help her.

When she was seventeen she was offered a job teaching very young children. She found that she liked to teach almost as much as she liked to study. Gradually, she began to dream of a school of her own—a school for girls.

It took time for that dream to come true. She had other posts as a teacher. She met and fell in love with and married a doctor, John Willard.

John Willard liked Emma's dream. He encouraged her to work out a plan for a woman's college, where young women could learn some of the same things that young men did in their colleges.

A *college* for women? In 1820, there was no such thing in the world. Emma showed her plan to various men who could be helpful in making it come true. They were horrifed by it. They were sure that if women tried to learn the same subjects young men did, their health would be ruined and they would not be good wives and mothers. Emma decided that it was a mistake to call her dream school a college. She gave it a new name—a female seminary.

Finally, Emma managed to interest the people of Troy, New York, in having a female seminary in their town. They never expected, nor did Emma, that the school she started would soon be the wonder of the city. Girls came from all

over New York, from Vermont, Massachusetts, and Ohio to attend Emma's school. The people of Troy saw them out walking every afternooon. They saw them at different churches on Sunday.

And then, at the end of the school year, Emma arranged a show—a public examination of the girls that went on for eight days. The parents and friends of the girls were invited. So were college professors, congressmen, and preachers. The big hall in the seminary building was crowded.

Emma Willard sat at a long table in the center, along with other teachers and guests. Then the girls came in, two by two. They carried little blackboards on which they drew maps of Europe, America, or the ancient world. They stood, side by side, as the teachers asked them questions. Sometimes the testing was interrupted and some girl played the piano or harp, or all the girls sang together.

The audience applauded and marveled. Plainly, these girls were still happy and well. Their health had not been ruined. Perhaps what they had learned *would* make them better wives and mothers, as Emma said.

The yearly examinations at the Troy Female Seminary went on, year after year. Dozens, then hundreds, of young women were graduated. And gradually, a new feeling about the education of girls began to grow in the United States. Other educated, intelligent women started colleges for girls. Mary Lyon founded what is now known as Mount Holyoke College. But Emma Willard, who had once argued that education was *silly* for girls, had been the real pioneer.

Ernestine Rose *(1810-1892)*

She Argued With a King

Every day Ernestine listened to her father say his prayers. Every day she heard him give thanks that he had not been born a woman.

One day, she had to ask, "Why? What is wrong with being a woman?"

Her father was angry that she dared to question a prayer that Jewish men had said for centuries. "Nothing is wrong with being a woman," he said. "It is simply better to be a man."

Ernestine said, "But that does not seem fair."

Her father said, "Be quiet. Who are you to say what is fair or unfair?"

Who was she, indeed? She was Ernestine Potowski, the young daughter of a rabbi in a little town in Poland. But it

seemed she was also a person who could not keep still when anything seemed wrong or unfair to her.

She grew older, and kept asking questions. Finally, after her mother died, her father decided that Ernestine needed a husband. One day he told Ernestine that he had arranged a marriage for her. Ernestine asked the man's name, and then said, "Father, I am sorry, but you must tell the man I cannot marry him. I do not love him."

Her father said, "I will do no such thing. The contract is already signed, the dowry promised."

Ernestine said, "I did not sign any contract. If you will not tell him that there will be no marriage, then *I* will."

Ernestine went to the man's house and did so. He said, "You are breaking the contract, and so I will still claim the dowry that your father promised me."

Ernestine thought about this for a while. Then she decided to take the matter to law and speak as her own lawyer.

For a young Jewish woman in Poland to do such a thing was unheard of. But Ernestine Potowski was so intelligent and made it so clear that it would be unfair for the man to keep her dowry, that the court ruled in her favor. She could keep her dowry and did not have to marry a man she did not love.

Before long, Ernestine left her father's house and went to live in Berlin, in Germany. Soon she learned that there were rules against Polish Jews living there.

Why should that be, she wondered. She went to the king himself to find out. The king was so surprised and impressed that he told this unusual young woman that *she* could stay in Germany as long as she wished.

But restless Ernestine was soon traveling on — to England. Here she met a group of people who were devoting their lives to speaking out against laws and customs that seemed unfair. Suddenly, Ernestine realized that this was what she wanted to do with her life also.

She fell in love with a man, William Rose, who thought just as she did. Soon they were married. Together they decided that the United States might be the best place to speak out for the changes that were needed in the world. So they sailed for America.

They were excited by New York City. It was so big and colorful and busy. But they soon saw the unhappiness and injustices there. They saw the rich taking advantage of the poor, the whites taking advantage of the blacks, and men treating women unfairly in many ways.

It happened that just then, a New York senator was trying to pass a bill in the legislature to provide that when women were married they could keep control of any money or property they owned.

So Ernestine Rose began her life in America going from door to door, asking women to sign a paper saying that they were in favor of the bill. Ernestine was surprised that so few women were interested. She asked them if they liked having no more rights before the law than children, idiots, and lunatics.

Finally, because Ernestine, and other workers also, would not give up, the bill was passed. But it had taken years.

By that time, Ernestine had begun to give lectures in public. This was something few women dared to do. When Ernestine came out on a platform, the men in the audience booed and jeered. But Ernestine waited until they were quiet

and then began to talk. Sometimes she spoke about the unfair way women were treated. Sometimes she spoke about the unfairness of slavery. Very few people wanted to hear such talk, but Ernestine was such a good speaker that they listened in spite of themselves.

The years went by, and as Ernestine Rose traveled back and forth across the country, giving her lectures, people gradually began to feel that women — well, some women, anyway — could speak in public without disgrace. They also began thinking more seriously about some of the laws and customs in America that kept it from truly being "the land of the free."

Ernestine Rose spent thirty-three years traveling and speaking in the United States. Then she and her husband went back to England to live. But the daughter of a Polish rabbi who could not help speaking out against anything that seemed unfair had left a lasting mark on her adopted country.

Elizabeth Blackwell *(1821-1910)*

Into Med School by Student Vote

She was in love and wished that she were not. The young man was handsome, healthy, and wealthy, and loved her too. But Elizabeth Blackwell was sure that they would not be happy long if they were married. The young man did not care at all about many things that she, her parents, and brothers and sisters considered important.

He was not troubled by slavery. He was not worried if others were overworked, poor, or in need. He simply wanted an easy life, with Elizabeth by his side.

"Marry me," he said.

Elizabeth knew that she must say no, but somehow she kept putting off the moment. She was still hesitating when a woman friend became very sick. Elizabeth spent many hours taking care of her.

One day the friend said, "It is so comforting to have a woman taking care of me. If only *women* were doctors." Then she looked at Elizabeth. "If only *you* were a doctor," she said.

Elizabeth was astonished.

"Why not?" the friend went on. "You have a wonderful mind. You learned Latin and Greek and mathematics with your brothers. Why shouldn't you study medicine?"

Elizabeth said, "But no woman has ever done so. Besides, who would teach me?"

Still, she was thinking that it *would* be exciting to try. She had always liked a challenge, a hard problem in geometry, a difficult piece for the piano, a stiff hike up a mountain. To try to become a doctor would make all the other challenges seem easy. And certainly it would keep her so busy she would have no time to think about the young man she knew she should not marry.

She said good-bye to him at last, and put away the flowers he had given her. Then she wrote letters to doctors all over the country, asking for advice. Only a few answered her. They said she was foolish to try to become a doctor, but if she insisted she would have to go to medical school.

Elizabeth began teaching piano in a school for girls to earn money for medical school. She found a doctor who let her read his books and who set up a course of study for her.

After she had worked and saved for two years she wrote to the best medical schools in the country, asking to be admitted. The answers that came back were all the same. Not one of the schools would accept a woman.

She wrote to some smaller schools, not so well known. Then, at one school, in Geneva, New York, the president decided to let the students vote on whether or not they wanted a woman as a fellow student.

As a joke, the students voted yes. They did not expect Elizabeth Blackwell to really come and study with them. But she did. The young men were astonished

when she appeared, small, pretty, and very quiet too.

All through the school year they watched her as she listened to the lectures and took notes. At the end of the year, they were not surprised when she did best in the exams. At the end of the

next year, she was graduated at the head of the class.

Still, she thought she needed more training, so she went abroad to France and then to England. She had trouble in both countries being accepted in medical schools, but she persisted until she *was*. Then she came back to America to start practicing in New York City.

Her first difficulty was in renting a room for an office. No one wanted to rent a room to a *woman* doctor. Finally, she rented a whole floor of a building.

Then, no patients came. Instead, people up and down the street began saying that a crazy woman was pretending to be a doctor. Surely anyone foolish enough to go to her would be poisoned.

Elizabeth offered free treatment to anyone who was too poor to go elsewhere for help. Gradually, as she healed those who came to her, others began to trust her. She was Doctor Blackwell at last, and she had broken the trail for other women to follow her.

Her own younger sister was studying medicine now. When she finished her training she joined Elizabeth. Together, they won the support of some intelligent people who helped them set up a hospital where anyone in need could come for treatment.

Elizabeth supervised the hospital and helped teach other women to become doctors. She was happy that she had made the choice she had, long before, and taken on the difficult challenge to become the first woman doctor in America.

Elizabeth Cady Stanton *(1815-1902)*

Declaration Against Injustices to Women

Banished! Sent upstairs to the gallery and seated behind a screen. The women who had come from America to England to be part of a great antislavery meeting were not going to be allowed to be part of it after all.

Young Elizabeth Cady Stanton, who

was on her honeymoon, was usually full of laughter. But she was not laughing now. She talked to Lucretia Mott, a Quaker woman who had become her friend.

"It is all so wrong," Elizabeth said. "We fight to end the slavery of black

people, but as women we are treated like slaves ourselves."

Lucretia Mott said, "You are right. Unless we marry good and generous men, as you have, my dear, and I, we have no voices, no power, no place, except in the kitchen, or up in the gallery like this."

Elizabeth said, "We should do something about it. When we get home we should have a meeting of *women*, to talk together about how to end *our* slavery."

Lucretia Mott nodded. "You are right, my dear. Let us do just that."

But after their return to America, Elizabeth was busy having babies and raising a family. She was helping her husband in his career and in his work against slavery. Lucretia and her husband were also busy in the antislavery fight.

Then, in the spring of 1848, some of Elizabeth's friends were visiting her at her home in Seneca Falls, New York. They talked, as they so often did, about the special, and not very happy, place in which women were supposed to stay.

Suddenly Elizabeth said, "Why are we waiting? Let's have that meeting of women. Let's have it right here in Seneca Falls in June."

Elizabeth's friends stared. "Yes," they said. "Yes, it's time."

"We will send out a call," Elizabeth said. "We'll put announcements in the papers and write letters to all the women we know."

Then she and her friends began to plan a program for the meeting. Elizabeth thought of the Declaration of Independence, written by Thomas Jefferson, seventy-two years before. She began to rewrite that Declaration to make it apply to women.

"We hold these truths to be self-evident," she wrote, "that all men — and *women* — are created equal . . . " She went on: "The history of mankind is a history of repeated injury . . . of man toward woman. . . . "

Then, just as the Declaration had listed all the complaints that the colonies had against England's rule, Elizabeth listed some of the complaints that women had against men. She wrote that women had no vote . . . no property rights . . . no rights over their children . . . no rights in their own persons . . . and so on, to a total of eighteen.

The great day of the meeting arrived. Women — and men too — came crowding into Seneca Falls. Carriages and buggies rattled down Main Street to the hall where the meeting was to be held.

Suddenly, Elizabeth was a little frightened. Was her Declaration too daring? All of the women became nervous. The hall was filling up. They had not expected such a crowd. People were greeting each other and waiting for the meeting to begin.

All at once it was time for Elizabeth to read her "Declaration of the Sentiments of Women." Her voice was very low as she began, but gradually it grew stronger. At last she was reading clearly and proudly. When she finished, everyone in the hall cheered.

There was much excited talk after that. People reminded each other that the first Declaration had led to a revolution. They wondered if this Declaration of the women could lead to another one — not a bloody one, but still one that would win women their freedom. They made plans about what to do next.

A few days later, they were shocked to read stories in newspapers across the country making fun of some foolish women who wanted a "Reign of Petticoats." These stories made many men snort and laugh, but actually, they did no harm. Many women read them and began to think and wonder.

Elizabeth and her friends had more meetings. They wrote letters and articles. A number of clever, thoughtful women joined them. One was Susan Anthony, who became Elizabeth's good friend. They all became more daring about speaking in public as Ernestine Rose had done. Soon they had an organization of women with members across the country. Elizabeth, along with Susan

Anthony, became one of the leaders of the organization.

She had a busy life, for she was a good mother to her eight children and a devoted wife also. She kept on fighting against slavery too, until that was ended by the Civil War. When black men were given the vote after the war, Elizabeth thought that women should have it also. But most of the men in the country still did not agree. So she, and Susan Anthony, and a host of other women kept up their fight.

Women, they said, were people first of all. Men had no right to banish them to kitchens, or galleries behind screens. If the fight was not won in their lifetime, Elizabeth, Susan, and all the others, were sure it would be won some day.

Harriet Beecher Stowe *(1811-1896)*

She Helped Abolish Slavery

"Wish Hattie had been a boy," her father
said, whenever his middle daughter did
or said something that showed how quick
and intelligent she was.

Piling up wood in the woodshed, arguing about questions of the day at the dinner table, writing prize-winning compositions in school — young Harriet Beecher could often do better than her brothers and sisters, though they were all quick and bright.

So when Lyman Beecher said, "Wish Hattie had been a boy," Harriet was not hurt. She knew her father loved her and was proud of her. He wished she was a

boy so that she could grow up to be a preacher, like he was. Lyman Beecher was sure that preachers were the only people with real power and influence.

But what kind of power did women have? If a woman was married, she might have a little influence on her husband and children. But if she did not get married — then what? Well, she could teach in a school for girls. Schools for girls were something new. Harriet's oldest sister, Catherine, had started such a school in Hartford, Connecticut. By the time Harriet was fifteen, she was not only studying at Catherine's school, she was teaching some classes as well.

When Lyman Beecher decided to move west to Cincinnati, Ohio, to preach and teach, Catherine went along to start a girls' school there. And of course Harriet went along too.

Cincinnati was across the river from Kentucky, a southern state where slavery was the law. The Beechers had always been against slavery, but now Harriet saw for herself what a cruel thing slavery was. She knew that her father could preach powerful sermons against it. So could her brothers, who had become ministers. They could vote in elections also, trying to elect men to make new laws. But what could she do? Nothing.

The years went by. She married a professor named Calvin Stowe. The babies began to arrive. She was busy from morning till night, keeping house and tending the children. But Calvin Stowe earned very little, so Harriet began to write stories for women's magazines. She was happy when she sold one for even a few dollars.

She still grieved about the evils of

slavery. Once she and Calvin helped a runaway slave to escape. But that did not seem like much.

Calvin got an offer to teach in the East. So he, Harriet, and the children moved to Maine. It was a time when the quarrel between the North and the South over slavery was causing angry feelings everywhere. The antislavery societies in the North had done so much writing and preaching that the people of the South were ready to leave the Union.

To please the Southerners, Congress passed a law making it a crime to help a slave escape. Harriet was shocked by this law. There was still nothing she could do — except, perhaps, she could write a story that might make people see that *of course* anyone who was held as a slave would try to escape.

She began to write and the story kept growing and growing in her mind. She wrote about a slave named Tom, who was sold away from his family, and about a beautiful slave named Eliza, who ran away with her young son when he was to be sold to a new master.

The story appeared in installments in a religious magazine. It began to attract attention right away. Soon it was published as a book. And then — suddenly — it seemed that everybody in America was reading *Uncle Tom's Cabin*.

The feelings that Americans had against slavery and for it were raised to fever pitch by this book. Soon the North and South were at war over the question of whether any man had the right to own another.

During the war, Harriet Beecher

Stowe visited President Lincoln at the White House, to ask when he was going to free the slaves.

"So this is the little woman who started this big war," he said. Of course, she alone had not started it, but her book had done a great deal to make people realize what they felt.

"Wish she were a boy," her father had said. But his middle daughter, so bright and quick, a woman, a wife and mother, had finally had more power and influence than any of his preacher sons.

Clara Barton *(1821-1912)*

A One-Woman, Mobile Army Hospital

She heard the news as she walked down the street in Washington, D.C. "Foreign troops are coming in this afternoon."

Clara Barton was puzzled. *Foreign* troops? Who could they be? Then someone told her that a Massachusetts regiment was returning in defeat from a battle in Virginia.

At first, Clara was shocked that anyone could call Massachusetts men *foreign*.

Then she reminded herself that Washington was really a Southern city. And in this Civil War, some people there did think of Northerners as their enemies.

Next Clara wondered if anyone she knew might be among the troops. Massachusetts was her home state. She had taught school there for ten years before she came to Washington to get a job as a copyist in the Patent Office. Perhaps some of the boys she had taught might be coming.

Suddenly, she was hurrying to the railroad station. When she got there, the troop train had just pulled in. Young men in dusty, torn, blue uniforms were getting off the train. Some were bandaged. Some used crutches. Clara saw that she knew several of them. They came to her, delighted to see her.

"Are you hungry?" she asked. "Is there anything you need that I can get?"

They were hungry, they said, and thirsty. There were a number of things that they needed — fresh bandages, handkerchiefs, paper, pens, tobacco.

Clara found out where they were to be quartered. She hurried to her rooming house. The woman who kept the rooming house helped Clara to fill baskets with food, to fill jugs with coffee, and to tear up sheets for bandages. Then Clara went out and found some porters to help her transport her supplies.

Because there was no other place for them, the soldiers were quartered in the Senate Chamber of the Capitol building. Clara came in with her food and other comforts. The men cheered as they saw her. Soon those with wounds had fresh bandages. Everyone had something to eat and drink. Then Clara read aloud to them from a Massachusetts newspaper which was some days old but still had news for the soldiers.

Clara had not planned it, but after that first effort to bring food and comfort to tired, wounded men, she was soon spending all her time at it. The Battle of Bull Run was fought not far away. Later, trainloads of soldiers were brought to Washington. Again, Clara took the men food, drink, and other needs.

The army had not yet organized its hospitals or medical services very well. Everything that Clara did was needed and appreciated by the soldiers. She wrote letters for the men. She put ads in the papers of Northern towns, asking the women there to send her supplies.

Soon, linens, blankets, preserved food, and liquors, and many other things came flooding in. The women were very glad to have someone to whom they could send such comforts for their men. Clara had to rent a warehouse to store the supplies.

Clara decided she could be even more

helpful if she could be at the battlefields. She knew some important men in Washington, because of her work at the Patent Office. She managed to get papers that allowed her to take a wagon, full of supplies, right up to the battle lines.

The first time that she came to the scene of a battle, she found that the army doctors had run out of almost everything they needed. She gave out the bandages and food she had brought. She helped the doctors as they tended the soldiers. She went out into the fields and gave the wounded men who were lying there gruel, or beef tea, or wine, and made them as comfortable as possible.

After that first trip, she went to battlefields again and again and always seemed to arrive when she was most needed. She helped Southern soldiers as well as Northern, feeding them, comforting them, writing letters for them. Many soldiers had heard about her by this time. They called her "The Angel of the Battlefield."

Army doctors and nurses were running regular army hospitals by now, but the personal care that Clara gave was still welcome. By the time the Civil War was over, Clara Barton had become famous. She was also tired and decided to rest by taking a trip to Europe. She arrived in the midst of a war between France and Germany. Her tiredness left when she found that once again she could help people in need. She could bring needed things to wounded men. She could help ordinary citizens too, who were homeless or hungry because of the war.

In Europe, Clara heard about a new

organization. Many countries had become members of it. The one aim of this organization was to bring aid to people who were suffering because of war, no matter what side they were on. It was called the Red Cross. All the countries that belonged to the Red Cross promised that its help could go anywhere with no interference.

Clara was astonished that the United States was not a member of this international organization. "But it must join," she thought. "It must." So Clara Barton came back to the United States, to lecture, to write, to meet with politicians, and to work tirelessly, year after year.

Finally, mostly because of her efforts, the United States did become a member of the Red Cross. Now, when everyone relies on Red Cross help in time of disaster or emergency, we can be grateful to Clara Barton, who went out on her own to bring aid to soldiers in the Civil War.

Victoria Woodhull *(1838-1927)*

First Woman to Run for President

"Victoria for President!"

A thousand men and women were crowded into a big hall in New York City. They were cheering and shouting for the woman whom they had nominated as

their candidate to be President of the United States.

On the platform, a slender, beautiful woman waited for the noise to die down before accepting the nomination.

A woman for President? Was it possible? Had things changed so much since the Civil War? Had those women who argued for women's right to vote finally won their goal?

No — women were no closer to having the vote than they had been. But Victoria Woodhull had announced that she was a candidate even so. She liked to do unusual and daring things. She liked to have people notice her.

"Crazy," the other children had called her when she was a little girl. "She's crazy. She sees visions and hears voices."

And it was true. Victoria did think that

she saw visions and heard voices, promising her wealth and fame, and telling her that one day she would be a ruler of her people. It did not seem possible that anything like that could happen to Victoria. Her family was poor and not very honest. She had a number of brothers and sisters who were hot-tempered and thoughtless.

And yet — when Victoria and a younger sister, Tennessee, came to New York they became friends of a rich man, Commodore Vanderbilt. Soon Commodore Vanderbilt helped them to set up a broker's office on Wall Street.

Victoria and Tennessee were written about in all the newspapers. They were the first women brokers in America. They made enough money so that they could start their own newspaper. In the newspaper, they and their friends wrote about all the reforms they thought were needed. Many people thought the newspaper was terrible. But there were others who thought it said things that needed saying.

Victoria found more important friends. One of them, a Senator, made it possible for her to speak to Congress on the right of women to vote. Victoria Woodhull was the first woman to speak before a Committee of Congress. After that, the leaders of the women's groups, Elizabeth Cady Stanton, Susan Anthony, and many others, became her friends. She too became a leader in the organization working to win women the right to vote. She began lecturing in towns across the country.

Then she decided that one way to make everyone realize that women should be taken seriously was to run for President. She announced in her newspaper that she was a candidate.

For a while, it seemed to Victoria that all the wonders she had been promised by the voices she heard when she was young were coming true. She had wealth. She was famous. Now a crowd was cheering her and asking her to be "ruler of her people." But how many would vote for her on election day?

Before that day came, Victoria, always rushing to do something no one else dared to do, published the details of a scandal about a minister in her newspaper. Respectable people everywhere turned against her.

On election day, she and her sister, Tennessee, were in jail. They had been arrested for sending indecent material through the mails. It was the end of any hope that Victoria would have even one vote for President.

Victoria and Tennessee lost most of their friends and had hard times for a while. Then they went to England. There they both married rich husbands and lived happily to old age.

Before long, the excitement and the anger that they had stirred up in the United States were forgotten. But because Victoria, following her visions, had dared to do some things that women had never done before, she had made it easier for other women to try the same things later.

Today, there are a number of women brokers. Today, women not only speak to Congress, but are members of Congress. Since Victoria's day, several women have run for President. But she was first.

Nellie Bly *(1867-1922)*

One-Woman Race Against Time

"Everybody is talking about that new book, *Around the World in Eighty Days*," said the prim and pretty young woman who signed her newspaper stories, Nellie Bly.

Her editor looked up and said, "That's right. What about it?"

Nellie — whose real name was Elizabeth Cochrane — said, "What if I

should go around the world in *less* than eighty days? That would make a good story, wouldn't it?"

The editor stared at her. "You? Go around the world?"

Nellie nodded. "Yes. But I'll try to go faster than the man in the book. Think of

the stories I can send back as I race against time!"

The editor smiled. "The readers might really go for that," he said.

Nellie said, "How soon can I start?"

The editor stopped smiling. "You? But you can't do it, Nellie. You're a woman, and a very young one too. How old are you, anyway?"

Nellie said, "I'm twenty-two. But that has nothing to do with it. Neither does the fact that I'm a woman. You know that I can go any place to get a story. Haven't I stayed days in prison? Haven't I lived in an insane asylum? Haven't I been down in mines? Why can't I go around the world?"

The editor shook his head. "It won't do, Nellie. It's a job for a man."

Nellie looked at the editor. "If you

send a man out on this job, I'll start out at the same time and race *him*."

The editor had learned something about Nellie's determination. He did not argue any more. "How soon can you be ready?" he asked.

Three days later, Nellie Bly was boarding a ship to sail from New York to Europe. The next day, her newspaper, *The World*, had a big story about the girl reporter who was going to try to beat the hero of the novel and go around the world in less than eighty days. Readers were interested at once. Nellie Bly had written exciting stories before. Now they waited for news that her ship had arrived in Europe.

As soon as she landed, she cabled a story to New York. Then she rushed for the train to take her on the next leg of her

journey. She traveled across France and down to Italy, sending back a story at every stop. Then she was boarding a ship to sail eastward across the Mediterranean.

By now, thousands of readers in America were looking at maps, following the route of Nellie Bly. And each day they read the latest news . . . of how Nellie rode a donkey through Port Said . . . how hot it was at the Suez Canal . . . how worried Nellie was when her ship was late getting to Ceylon.

They also read about the strange sights Nellie was seeing—mountains, and rivers, and temples, camels, elephants, and jewels. From Canton, China, Nellie wrote that she had bought a monkey that sat on her shoulder. Finally, she was in Japan and boarding the ship that would take her across the Pacific to America.

A fierce storm blew up at sea but Nellie only worried about the delay. The days of travel were mounting up. Would she make it back to New York before the deadline?

A crowd was waiting to greet her when she landed in San Francisco. Everyone cheered as the slender girl, in a long tweed cape, and a little cap, with a monkey on her shoulder, got off the ship. But a special train was waiting and Nellie hurried to board it. All across the country, people gathered at stations to see the train that was carrying Nellie Bly.

At last the train pulled into New York. Nellie Bly had traveled almost twenty-five thousand miles. She had gone around the world in seventy-two days, six hours, and eleven minutes. She had

broken the record of the book. The station was mobbed with cheering people. A carriage was waiting for her. Soon she was riding in a parade up Broadway.

Nellie Bly! Everyone talked about her. People said that she had begun The Age of Rapid Travel.

Less than a hundred years later, when jet planes go around the world in hours, Nellie's journey does not seem so rapid. But when she made the trip it was as exciting as man's first journey into space. And the fact that a young woman had made it simply added to the wonder.

Carrie Chapman Catt *(1859-1947)*

Women Win the Right to Vote

She was Carrie Lane, a bright and pretty thirteen-year-old, helping her mother wash the breakfast dishes.

"I'll finish up now," she said to her mother. "You go change your dress to go into town."

Her mother said, "I'm not going into town."

"Not going with father?" Carrie said. "But don't you want to vote for Mr. Greeley?"

Her mother said, "Yes, I would like to.

But women can't vote, Carrie."

Carrie stared at her mother. Somehow, in all the weeks before, when her mother and father had talked about how much they would like to have Horace Greeley as the next President, Carrie had never realized that her mother would not be voting along with her father.

"Women can't vote?" asked Carrie. "But that's not fair."

Her mother said, "I don't think so either. But that's how it is, and nothing seems likely to change it."

Carrie did not make any vow, then and there, that someday *she* would do something to change this unfair situation. She did argue about it with a boy who came

calling on her. He tried to defend the way things were, and when she kept arguing, he left.

Later, her father said to her mother, "I wish Carrie wouldn't go on that way. I'm afraid she'll never get a husband."

As it happened, Carrie did get a husband, soon after she graduated from college. She had gone on to be a high school principal when she met Leo Chapman. They fell in love and were married. Carrie gave up her other ambitions and only wanted to be a good wife.

Carrie and Leo were moving to San Francisco to start a new life there when Leo suddenly became ill, and died within a few days. Carrie felt that her life had no meaning. She took a job as a secretary, to fill her time.

One evening, she had to deliver some

papers to a businessman in his office. He signed the papers, then got up and put his arms around her. Carrie was horrified and pushed him away.

The man was surprised and angry. He said, "Why do you come into a man's world, then, if you don't want a little friendly attention?"

Carrie ran out of the office and hurried home through the dark streets. All the while, she was thinking, "Why should it be only a *man's* world? Can't a woman do a job and be given the same respect as a man?"

Suddenly she knew what she wanted to do. She wanted to work to help women win the right to be individuals, doing what they wanted. And it seemed to Carrie that the first thing women had to win was the right to vote.

She went back to Iowa, her home. She
joined the society organized so long ago
by Elizabeth Stanton and her friends —
the women's suffrage association.

Working for that cause became Carrie's life. She began to give lectures. She was a good speaker, both serious and funny. She helped plan campaigns and came to know all the important men in politics. Not many of them wanted to let women vote, but all admired and respected her.

She was married again, to an old school friend, George Catt. Now she was known as Carrie Chapman Catt. George Catt approved of her work, so Carrie kept on lecturing, writing, traveling, and meeting people. She joined societies in Europe which were also concerned with winning the vote for women.

Then, in 1914, the nations of Europe went to war. Carrie hoped that America could stay out of it, but finally that seemed impossible. After the United

States declared war, Carrie encouraged the women of America to help the war effort. Women took jobs in factories and offices, doing many things that only men had done before. They served as nurses. They sold bonds. They saved food.

Carrie did her part also, but all the while, she, and others with her, kept trying to win the vote. Gradually, as men in politics saw how much they needed the help of women to win the war, many decided that it might not hurt if women voted — just like men.

Finally, a year after the war was over, a bill was passed in Congress. The Constitution was amended so that a person's sex had nothing to do with the right to vote.

It had been seventy-two years since Elizabeth Stanton and her friends had written the Women's Declaration of Independence. Many women had lectured, written, and given years of their lives to the cause. Now, at last, the goal was won.

Women held a great victory celebration in 1920, after the 19th Amendment to the Constitution was approved. Women and schoolchildren across the country banded together to get a gift for the woman who had led the fight so long, Carrie Chapman Catt. One little boy thought that he was giving a penny to buy something for Charlie Chaplin's cat.

Carrie laughed when she heard that story. Everyone laughed. Everyone was happy. "We've won," Carrie cried to the women. "Be glad. Rejoice, applaud, and be glad!" And everyone was glad, and did rejoice.

And Then...

Did everything change for women after that year when they won the vote?

Quite a few women had become doctors by this time. Women were lawyers. Some were engineers, and there were many women reporters.

Through the years, women had always been actresses, dancers, or singers. Now those professions were considered more respectable.

Women were running businesses, publishing newspapers, flying airplanes.

Now that they were able to vote, women began to run for political office. The first woman Senator was elected. In 1932, President Roosevelt appointed the first woman Cabinet member, Frances Perkins.

Still, having the vote did not change things for all women as much as many had hoped it would. Many men still felt that women's place was in the home, taking care of them and the children. Many women were anxious to please men and would not try to do anything more.

The right to vote, it turned out, was just one step toward women being all that they could be.

Women—and men too—would have to keep on working to understand themselves and each other, before they both were free to be what they best could be.

About the Author

JOHANNA JOHNSTON found that writing biography was an enjoyable way to share her interest in history with young people. Many of her books dealt with the achievements of women and of blacks, among them *Together in America: The Story of Two Races and One Nation*; *A Special Bravery*; and *Paul Cuffee: America's First Black Captain*.

Her book *Thomas Jefferson, His Many Talents* won the Thomas Alva Edison Award for Excellence in 1962.

Johanna Johnston also worked as a staff writer for CBS Radio and Television in New York City, where she died in 1982. She had one daughter, Abigail.

SCHOLASTIC BIOGRAPHY

Available wherever you buy books, or use this order form.

Scholastic Inc., P.O. Box 7502, 2931 East McCarty Street, Jefferson City, MO 65102

Please send me the books I have checked above. I am enclosing $_____ (please add $2.00 to cover shipping and handling). Send check or money order — no cash or C.O.D.s please.

Name_____ Birthdate_____

Address_____

City_____ State/Zip_____

Please allow four to six weeks for delivery. Available in the U.S. only. Sorry, mail orders are not available to residents of Canada. Prices subject to change.   BIO695